The Crone at the Casino

The Crone
at the Casino

Janet McCann

Copyright © 2013 Janet McCann
All Rights Reserved

ISBN: 978-0-9850838-9-2
Library of Congress Control Number: 2013954492

Manufactured in the United States

Lamar University Press
Beaumont, Texas

For Hugh—
    48 Years and Counting

Poetry from Lamar University Press:
Alan Berecka, *With Our Baggage*
David Bowles, *Flower, Song, Dance*: Aztec *and Mayan Poetry* (a new translation)
Jeffrey DeLotto, *Voices Writ in Sand*
Mimi Ferebee, *Wildfires and Atmospheric Memories*
Ken Hada, *Margaritas and Redfish*
Michelle Hartman, *Disenchanted and Disgruntled*
Dave Oliphant, *The Pilgrimage, Selected Poems: 1962-2012*
Erin Murphy, *Ancilla*
Carol Reposa, *Underground Musicians*
Jan Seale, *The Parkinson Poems*

For information on these and other Lamar University Press books go to
www.LamarUniversityPress.Org

Other Books by Janet McCann Include

The Bell Jar by Sylvia Plath, editor and contributor
Creative and Critical Thinking, second edition, with W. Edgar Moore and Hugh McCann
Emily's Dress
In a Field of Words, with Sybil Estess
Looking for Buddha in the Barbed-Wire Garden
Odd Angles of Heaven: Contemporary Christian Poetry, coedited with David Craig
Place of Passage, Contemporary Catholic Poetry, coedited with David Craig
Poems of Francis and Clare co-edited with David Craig
Pascal Goes to the Races
Wallace Stevens Revisited: The Celestial Possible

CONTENTS

I. The Crone at the Casino

1	Crone Poet
3	Castiglion Fiorentino Saturday
5	Somnia
7	Buying a Bed at 65
9	In the Alzheimer's Ward
11	The Crone at the Austin Poetry Festival
13	At the Garage Sale
15	The Crone at the Casino
17	Six and a Half Ways of Looking at a Cat
19	Retirements in Late Spring
20	The Three Ages of Europe
21	Extractions
23	The Crone at the Catholic Conference
25	On the Grounds of the Monastery where Fra Angelico Painted
26	Galileo's Eye
30	Old Cinderella
31	Sylvia at Sixty
32	The Crone at the Cathedral
33	Laundry
34	Life List
35	The Bookstore on Broadway in Albany
37	The Autumn Name of God

II. A Cat Named Flaubert

- 41 Girly Restaurant in Texas
- 42 Invitation
- 43 Brit Lit 101
- 45 Nachdenken über Katzen
- 46 Cat's
- 47 Oatmeal Poem
- 49 Old House
- 51 Twitch
- 52 Sam's
- 53 Perhaps
- 54 The Home of the Radioactive Cats
- 56 "Girl Making a Garland"
- 58 Unsent Letter to a Long-Gone Friend
- 59 5 a.m.
- 61 My Son Requests a Typewriter
- 63 Flowering Cactus
- 64 Still
- 65 What to Do with the Remains
- 66 Facebook
- 67 Walking Home Late Sestina
- 69 Self-Inflating Pillow
- 70 Sound of No Hands Clapping
- 71 Doors That Don't Quite Shut
- 72 A Rose by Any Other Name Is Something Else
- 74 Solo
- 75 Review Copy
- 77 Explanation
- 79 Narrow Places

81 2012
82 Movement, Solitude, Space
84 At the Liendo
85 Sleeping Women in Movies
86 The Cat at the End of That Poetry Anthology
88 Monastery Cats

In every Animal that walks upright, the Deficiency of the Fluids that fill the Muscles appears first in the highest Part: The Face first grows lank and wrinkled; then the Neck; then the Breast and Arms; the lower Parts continuing to the last as plump as ever: So that covering all above with a Basket, and regarding only what is below the Girdle, it is impossible of two Women to know an old from a young one. And as in the dark all Cats are grey, the Pleasure of corporal Enjoyment with an old Woman is at least equal, and frequently superior, every Knack being by Practice capable of Improvement.

—Benjamin Franklin

I. The Crone at the Casino

Crone Poet

I don't have many nouns. You have to earn them,
can't look them up. My glasses are scratched and blurred,
too hard to see. Is it a bay-breasted warbler?

It may be, with its dark crown, its chestnut patches,
but I don't know, I haven't earned it. I look up at it
as it chirps at me from a branch. I identify it

tentatively from its *teesiteesiteesi* and the colors
but I have not mastered it, the way I did
the chipping sparrows, the purple martins

who do not come to the house I built especially
for them. I know them, their glossy beauty,
and they live here; one surprised me

on the roof's edge, but neat apartments built
according to their needs still fail to draw them.
Other nouns so much easier to tame:

words from computers, like *motherboard*
and *CPU*, sit around in my head
like coins from other countries, words from cooking

like *ghee* and *mirepoix* and *roux*
are burned into my skin by bubbling fats,
even the names of gods and mountains come,

but I want to chase the words around the yard
throwing arcs of breadcrumbs, sunflower seeds;
my stumbling feet startling them into flight.

Castiglion Fiorentino Saturday

Because I am missing a front tooth
and my dentist is 2000 miles away
I make friends with the person others call
the crazy catlady and who lacks
the same tooth. I sit next to her while she
feeds them; they come out of the bushes
around the bench. I have bought cat food too
but they won't come near me. I would
give my cat food to her but she says,
Just wait, put it out and wait. I do.
We sit and talk, *Have you been
doing this for a long time? Twenty
years or so, not long.* We converse
carefully because I have only got to
lesson five in the Italian book and it
doesn't really cover this situation, has more
to do with buying train tickets. Cats
(5 of them now) cluster around her feet,
eat up her food. *I have five of my own,*
she says, *my place is too small for any
more cats.* I know then she is not a crazy
catlady or she would have dozens. Her plate
is almost empty now, and finally
an orange longhair with bushy, matted
fur edges in my direction. Sniffs at the
plate. Digs in. And then all the others

join him, a ring of them, gobbling up
the pellets, conversing in cat,
which I understand at least as well as
I do Italian. Stunned with happiness,
I look at the catlady. She mirrors my smile.

Somnia

you sleep and the old dog sleeps,
       sometimes you think
you have slept up all the sleep,

and are tossing in dreams
   snatching at rags of blanket,
      your hips scraping at rocks.

nowhere is deep enough to stay there
   the dream shabby and fragile
your fingers poke through and touch the cold

the patter on the roof humdrum as fingers
   tapping on the dream-bar
     where your order never comes

though you wait for it in half-light
  and the other grainy-faced patrons
all seem to be served

the mattress hard and narrow
     no one even in dream
calling out your name

as you rise and fall in sleep,
    the old dog with you,
billows and hills of sleep.

Buying a Bed at 65

is different from buying one at 45
or 25.
The room of 100 beds quiet
except for the slick bed-salesman
who offers test drives.

I feel the firmnesses and softnesses,
lie back on one or two,
imagine a roomful of sleepers.
These are not playpens or trapezes,
they are not fantasy worlds, they are
places to sleep at night.

The salesman talks of arthritis
and swollen disks, how the Magic Fingers
soothe these. He doesn't speak of pleasure
but there's a young couple on the farthest bed
taking a few sly liberties.
His pitch will be different for them.
Now he looks away, deliberately not seeing
where their hands are.

The one we choose is medium
and he asks do we want the ten-year

warranty? I close my eyes.
Have we ten years left of sleep? From the corner come giggles from the Magic Fingers Mattress.

In the Alzheimer's Ward

Well-lit, a giant colorful playpen,
bright fish in huge aquariums
and tropical birds in cages big as windows.

Old children sit in wheelchairs
or on benches, one is curled up tight
in the beanbag chair, like a museum's

display of birth. A posted schedule
presumably for visitors and staff,
announces *3 o'clock, memory*.

After the television hour, after nap,
well before dinner, they will have memory.
This is the best Alzheimer's ward

in the country, a visitor
murmurs. Before nap, after television,
daily, comes memory. On each door

a photo, *Doris, Eunice, Dora May*
lives here, photos like those on Italian gravestones.
A sweet-faced woman sits with an armful of shoes:

*They have forgotten them, I will keep them
for them, they leave them everywhere.* Another
pulls at blotchy arms, says *Look what they did to me.*

But most are silent. Still, at three o'clock
they will have memory. At three o'clock
the memory cheerleader will come dancing in.

Mother, she will say slowly, gesturing,
Father. Home. Husband. Wife. Children.
But surely, surely it is better not to remember,

to look at the bright wings, the sleek fish,
to hold the teddy bears sitting around on tables
(that belong to no one in this communist country)

and to watch the clock hands move? But the memory
    cheerleader
comes, she will lead them. *Husband, mother, home.*

The Crone at the Austin Poetry Festival

patches of light and shade on the outside table
of the Austin café where this is happening

a train hooing in the middle of a line:
a caesura—a trembling voice picks up again

eyes closed, the crone still sees the flicker
of leaves blowing dark and light behind her lids

a sestina stops sharp at the end of every line
like a French chef is chopping it into segments

and she opens her eyes to a padlock and a screen
behind which other tables sit on an overgrown

lot, a café the mirror of this one, but abandoned
and silent, and she dreams herself gone over

beyond the screen, to the sunlit table
where now the 70s Austin poets she remembers

ghost the white chairs, David Yates, Jim Cody,
Joseph Colin Murphey; Susan Bright joins them

and they listen, smile and shake their heads
as if to say, that line is not quite right

but the *feel* of it is right, about the war
and hunger, the strange American lack of love

shadow-arms raise glasses of blue wine
to toast each other, and the crone wonders

when, what day, she'll find herself among them,
at those other tables, listening in full sun

At the Garage Sale

I found a View-Master
with all the scenes of my childhood,
places we did not go, but saw in books,

Grand Canyon, Las Vegas, tea-gardens
of San Francisco, and the images too
were old, signs and motels suggested fifties.

I wanted to find my father's dog with wheels,
the stone blocks that had been his
with their tiny carved doors and windows.

I wanted to find a whirling sparkler,
a summer afternoon at the beach, a dripping
ice-cream cone, my brother running

down the shore with a big dog. I wanted to find
that day on Coney Island, a box
of Cracker-Jack with a real toy, maybe

a Scottie dog. I wanted one deep breath
of cotton-candy and cigarette smoke,
hairspray and cheap perfume. I wanted to fly,

hover over the house the way I used to,
look in my window at me asleep. The View-Master
was smaller than I'd thought, its pictures

too bright and rough, like children's pop-up books.

The Crone at the Casino

Always the cloud of people drifts
in the streets, in blinking rooms, around
the nickel machines. What do we want,
youth, money, fun, the buzz of lights
and drug of neon, here where strangers
tell you their lives in elevators?

Is this the 50's? Did we stumble
through the wrong door into 1954?
It is possible, possible. So many people
bear odd-shaped drinking containers
smelling of fruit and cheap rum. Towers
shadow streets, cars creep along the strip.

Panel trucks advertise half-dressed
women "who want to meet YOU!"
And the tee-shirts in the downtown—
shaved head wears Darth Vader,
crone wears "real lucky" in jewels,
2 tubby grandmas just like me

wear body-length tees imprinted with
young, buff bodies. This is the place
of any illusion you could want,

you don't even have to pretend to believe it.
Hotels' anonymous friendliness
without contact, built to house thousands

and move them along. Though it is late
the bells still ring, the lights swirl,
winners scream, electricity pulses
in her fingertips. Does what happens
here stay here as they promise,
or do we take bright pieces of it home?

Six and a Half Ways of Looking at a Cat
(with apologies, of course, to Wallace Stevens)

I
Zen puss–
paw prints as
absences.

II
The eye of the cat is moving,
something must be flying.

III
Don't think of golden birds!
A metallic squawk,
then silence.

IV
The letters moved ecstatically
across the screen,
until a dark form leapt.

V
After dark all cats are gray
except this one,
the invisible.

VI
The cat likes poetry,
she preens herself
to the accents of Poe.

VI ½
An old woman and a cat are one.

Retirements in Late Spring

People moving out of their offices on Saturday.
Carts full of books tugged down almost vacant halls.
A child shrieks, a flurried argument arises.

People moving out of their offices on Saturday
While a few of us hide behind our closed doors
Staring at computer screens, fiddling with tasks

And feeling envious of those who are going
Away, willingly or unwillingly.
People falling out of trees on Saturday.

People falling out of the sky on Saturday,
Little Magritte-men with briefcases

Descend like snow on the hallways of my mind.
The noise is not a racket but a murmur
Of things changing. I am getting old,

As I tap the keyboard brown spots grow
On my hand, veins protrude that should not be there.
People moving out of their offices on Saturday.

On Saturday, people moving out of the world.

The Three Ages of Europe

Young she was an explorer
jumping nude into languages and oceans
sharing strange vehicles with stranger men
learning European words for hangover:
Katzenjammer, gueule de bois, resaca

Middle-age made of her a traveler
riding the metros without a map
sitting on concrete jetties
eating prosciutto and melon
dangling her feet in the Mediterranean

But now she's just a tourist
following the guide with red umbrella
who herds her along with other sheep
to the bus, or to the chosen bistro where
ready baguettes and coffees line the bar

Extractions

four hours in the chair,
you rise bleeding,
teeth tiny bumps in the tray—

not the nightmare teeth
that gleamed at you from
corners of dream-rooms

but the bleak gray reality,
pain upon waking,
shaking hands and an unsteady floor.

thank you, you say so carefully
reaching for checkbook.
they will repair you later,

another day and repaint your face.
you feel violated.
small deaths, those bumps

like fetuses. you wish someone
would bring you soup, condole.
dizziness pushes your car

to the right, on the short
drive home. animals darting
into the brush look healthy,

toothy, feral. your house awaits.
you stare at mirrors. happy without reason,
you beam your Gothic smile.

The Crone at the Catholic Conference

popcorn in a yellow machine with a red lid
I think of barrel-organs and monkeys

street dancers and tinny music
but this is a conference on the soul

in all the rooms left and right off this one
they are talking, talking, talking about the soul

the priests' and nuns' and brothers'
voices join in the hallway like old ghosts

the popcorn smells of butter
of old movies with Sydney Greenstreet

and Peter Lorre, its rich oily scent
slips under doors of conference rooms

where you are against Cartesian dualism
or you are not, are for it, you blind fool

long-ago summer afternoons gather
in shadows on the marquetry, under statues

the university is old, weathered, romantic
panes rattle in the sudden wind

outside fallen leaves whirl and drift
and we count, *body, body, body, soul*

On the Grounds of the Monastery Where Fra Angelico Painted

vietato entrare nel gardino

tree and dead plants,
sparse patches of grass
brick-lined paths from ancient arch to arch
anonymous weeds

ne pas entrer dans le jardin

cigarette butts
from scofflaws, maybe the groundskeeper
scraggly pansies, circle
of bricks around a barren tree trunk

der eintritt in den garten ist verboten

rusty pump off to the left
no songbirds would come here,
Eden stripped for the movers
pebbles mingle with dirt in tepid sunlight

do not enter into the garden

Galileo's Eye

In the Cafe of the Planets
   Galileo's eye
stares through centuries

the eye red-veined
   tired from seeing
wide under reddish lid

My own eyes weighted
  old and sleepy
Galileo looks at me

his truth hanging there
  opaque, not transparent
perpetually revolving

the abstract beauty of machines
 their gold gleam
an astrolabe tells the light

secrets he deciphered
  folding up again around
other centers

clutching
   other secrets
to their hearts

* * *

boys swimming in a lake by a bridge
in a female season
shoulders touched by zephyrs

moon-drawings startling in their precision
the pencil tracing the phases
a language of symbols

so that 500 years later
an old woman gasps, says, *yes that is it*
that is the moon

* * *

"The Bible teaches how to go to heaven,
not how the heavens go"
he wrote to the Grand Duchess Christina.

Of course the Inquisition
stopped by,
sniffing for heresy,

and scenting it. Galileo's eye
did not wish to veil itself
or glance away, but he had to

look aside, askance
you cannot look the Inquisition
in the eye and live

he did not truly say
"but it still moves"
after the decree, though still it did

* * *

In Galileo's dream one daughter, the beautiful nun
who loves him whole-souledly, prays for him every day,
tells him at last the secret names of the numbers.

He knows it all, then, everything comes together
the way no one had ever even dreamed it,
the system, his understanding, a great clap of thunder.

* * *

Galileo was blinded by glaucoma,
not by looking at the sun
as was reported. The sun

did him no harm, nor did the moon and stars.

Grandmother guides grandson to the telescope,
shows him how to use it. He catches his breath
at the curve, the long unscrolling
of heaven.

Old Cinderella

Arthritic fingers fasten the diamond tiara
(That glass slipper in a case, backlit)

Prince long gone in a drunken duel
Over someone's daughter

Never wanted another, took up sewing
But now can't make the tiny stitches

Invites Drusilla, remaining stepsister
To the castle for tea

(Castle is entailed and will go
To her son)

Dru a retired washerwoman
With red hands

Will snag a bauble for the pawnbroker
Though Cindy gives her money

Cindy tells her granddaughter
Marry a carpenter

Sylvia at Sixty

After forty you don't think of knives,
they don't glitter seductively in drawers.
(Yesterday I cut my hand again,
an unexpected piece of sharp steel
when I tried to fix the fan. Blood dripped darkly
over the stilled blades. Only six stitches,
the novocaine hurt worst.)

She would have settled back into forms,
the blood-jet stilled, her craft fine-tuned by reading.
She would have always been the guest-lecturer
who was nervous, complained about the room
but gave a great speech.
She would have been read, but more like Donald Justice.

Her final housemate would have been
an airedale. She would have been most careful
about his health. Her children and grandchildren
would visit now and then, but not stay long.

Gardening, birds in the garden, grackles, sparrows,
jays and wrens. Purple marten feeder
above the sweetpeas, no more angry bees.
Daddy, old ghost,
can't call me now.
Anyway, I'll join you soon enough.

The Crone at the Cathedral

Bell ringing violently
Huge bells jumping in the tower
Curves of metal scaring off the pigeons

And rain cuts the breath
As I kneel at wooden pew
Among dark-clad elders in first light

Mumble prayers in another language
And take the candle my neighbor
Gives me, hold it in my palm

The cylinder, the bright point of light
And I don't know what it is for
But desire is returning, though the church

Is cold, amidst the prayers
Of centuries, and the smell of old stone
And dust, and the statues

Worn shiny in places by touching,
And the incense, curl of gray smoke,
And desire, that dove in the groin, returning

Laundry

So many clotheslines hanging in sun, rain
or snow, whites, blues, dingy along the tracks
or bright in fields, between tall buildings in cities,

reflecting the day's mood: grey, acid,
brilliant, inspired. I don't see anyone hang it up
but there it is, a statement, this is my life

for all to read. And now it is my turn,
with arthritic fingers I clip slips, sweaters,
shirts to the line. Will it freeze,

will the wind shatter it to ribbons?
A haphazard poet, I am careful with this,
my lines must be even, come to full stops.

Blouses in front, sweatshirts, heavy towels
in back, the damp fabric of them
weighing down the cord. I step away,

rub chilled, stiff hands, remember all the wearings,
smudges of work, of sweat, wrinkles and crumplings
erased now, look at the clean lines.

Life List
    in memory of S. A.

My friend the scholar-birdwatcher
is dying, after a quiet regular life
of Milton and birds, and if I could

imagine him a farewell, it would be this:
to look out into the small yard
he tended for forty years, to where

he placed the bird houses, the martin
house and the hummingbird feeder,
just in time to see a sweep of air

curve in and take form, the great arctic gyrfalcon
not on his life list, there on the sill,
to be recognized by beak, feathers and pinions

and final knowledge, Adam's homecoming
after the story's end, better than Eden.
May he have in his hand a feather, that his wife

might know where he has gone.

The Bookstore on Broadway in Albany: AWP Conference 1999

"The fate of poetry at the end of the print culture..."
—Mark Hillman

In the window, children's hardbacks
from the seventies, foxed spines,
ripped covers. Out front a rack
of faded fly-specked rain-spotted paperbacks.

It's almost dark in there, I make my way
among the racks and racks of crumbling
paperbacks, magazines, the precarious stacks
of books and music. Mouse dirt. Ants.

Dust over everything. At first the room
looks empty but then I spot an ancient
Irishman slumped on a rusty metal chair.
I find a Nero Wolfe for 35 cents

and give him two quarters. Once back
at the hotel, I stop to think,
maybe I missed a first edition Poe, or
a *Leaves of Grass* in there! So I return,

but the place is all closed up, a big
black padlock on the door. And I am glad,
for the long dark room was balanced at the point

between holding separate books and only dust

that would drift out through the city
in a sullen cloud, and finally disperse
to a tepid papery smell over Albany.
I should have known, passing over tinny quarters,

that our commerce took place there at the very edge,
that it was nightfall, that we were poised
between coherence and chaos,
between history and annihilation.

The Autumn Name of God

Color, said the nun, is the autumn
name of God
and his winter name is Silence

and here is how it is for us:

we have only color and silence left
the leaves burn beautifully in their slow dying
the wind through the branches
makes a music like a lullaby
it carries back the names of other seasons

autumn is the last color of the house

framed there at the end of the path
amidst brilliant oaks and maples
we don't see its peeling paint,
the way the shutter hangs by a hinge

reds and yellows blow across the path,
pile up against the wall

soon, bare branches and snow

the coming of silence
God's final name

II. A Cat Named Flaubert

Girly Restaurant in Texas

Leaves from the plant store
invade the patio,
grapple the bentwood chairs.
The menu is almost all quiche
and salad, I have a tiny
chicken breast glazed with
cranberries. So many women
outside, inside, buying begonias,
lobelias and little pots of
herbs for the kitchen garden, women
fumbling the windchimes, checking
their makeup in the wrought-iron
framed mirrors. Artificial cats
in apparent sleep dot the benches,
you have to touch one
to see she isn't real. I want a man
to shove his way in here
with a big golden retriever.
I want the dog to gobble up
the fake cats, the man to
holler for a Lone Star.
I want the waitresses
in their green elf suits
to run like hell.

Invitation

  You're not here, so I am having
shrimp in bed with the cats! The delicate remoulade
    running down my blue sleeve
as the pink crescents are dunked
   and downed—cats playing with tails,
    batting at shells—
is there shrimp in bed, in heaven? And if you were here—
   this is your bed, after all,
  these sheets your chosen sheets—
what would you say?
       The pillow slippery
with sauce, one cat leaping
   and pawing the air, the other curled on the quilt
with a slick pink sliver—
    I'm tossing the shells
waste-basketward heedless
    across the steamy redolent room—
Would you come in?
  Would you join me?

Brit Lit 101

Working in bed, surrounded by
books and pens and notebooks
and a flurry of penciled notes—working
into the late morning, while outside
the paper has long lain on the step
the trash has long gone with a rattle and clank
and you are there reading, working in bed
which leads to reverie, which leads to dream,
which leads—don't shut those eyes! The coffee cold
and the house empty, and yet you read
and write, thinking, remembering,
weaving the bits of thought into your work
and bits of work into the strands of thought
so that Chaucer's people take up residence
in the room with you—the Prioress, the Nun's
Priest, the Wife of Bath sitting right there
on the foot of the bed and trying on your robe,
saying, well, at least it's big enough
but it doesn't look like much, and the Friar
looking away because you're old and fat
and not worth fooling with, but the Pardoner
has something to sell you, to abate your sins,
you think it's one of those little umbrellas
they put on summer drinks, and not a relic.
There's Chaucer the Pilgrim, himself tubby
and jolly, and then when the phone
rings and they all vanish into corners

like so many cats, you lie there silent
in the bright ringing center, and do not answer.

Nachdenken über Katzen

"Big cats do not purr," the TV says.
Another negative fact, like Alligators
Do Not Have Tongues, and Elephants
Do Not Really Go
Anyplace Special to Die. I assume they mean
Really big cats, not my fifteen-pound
Alley tom, but tigers, panthers, jaguars.

Why cats?   This one is beautiful and mean,
Claws at my pen, my right hand is a red
Spiderweb because of him. No use
But for decor and mice. And then he doesn't
Hunt on my account. Cats kill more cleanly
Than Hemingway, and without that heavy
Symbolic freight. That's why cats, I guess,

But why facts then? Mother-Goddess has a lion
Rumbling in her lap, rubbing
His golden mane against her rounded thigh.
Panthers curl at her feet,
A buzz arises like a cave breathing.
Peace, sister, it is time now,
The violence all inside. It sleeps and purrs.

Cat's

in season! and the three-year-old
can't sleep for the trio of toms
howling in the hedge, their rough wails
of longing.
        Thinks it's a lost child
grown wild, calling to others in the woods,
the children who ran away, who swing on vines
parentless, live on nuts and berries, play
games in circles under the moon. It is one voice
heavy with a vibrancy of shadows
that rise and fall around it.
                      He listens long
and pulls himself upright on the crib bars
to look out into the moonlit yard
but does not cry or speak.

Oatmeal Poem

swirls of brown sugar, lumpy soup,
golden pools of butter.

no, you say, *no!*
not this!

the fireside, the cold walk to school.
have you got everything?

just gimme a granola bar.

the warm, sweet glue.
spooning it up. raisins.
sticky spoon, residue of gum
in the blue bowl.

look, not even the cat will eat it.

but I want you to swallow it all down,
my round window, the bed
plumped up, the afghan with green diamonds,
Betty and Peter waiting
at the end of the gravel walk.

you used to eat this stuff,
were you poor?

to swallow the taste
of sweet melted cardboard,
I will give you my silver spoon
with the rolled handle.
a whiff of kerosene.

are you ready now?
it's time to go.

Old House

of course mice, therefore cats.
       a great hunting in the dark,
    tiny squeaks of terror,
        little soft deaths.
shadows keep their hundred-year-old
 house at bay,
   tethered, though he says he hears
vacancy underneath, trembling
   under the oak floors.
wants to shore up the structure with new wood.

      the cats, kittens, half grown
drowse all day on the massive furniture,
    on the magazine, in the shadow of the candlesticks.

old house, painted and repainted
 a fiercely stippled white,
   shadows mixed in the tint,

leaves falling,
    seasons of sun and rain,
         peach trees in the field flowering,
fruit picked, fruit rotting in the grass,
     over and under,
the house floating on cloud,
  all night, dissolving, its colors peeling away,

behind the last forgotten shade, a form in air,
    the dream of the house.

Twitch

Twitch of the cat's tail. Alone's a stone, Grandmother said.
The we a pretty story,
we the couple, we the children, we the family, we the country.
My countrymen and women. My, my.
Grandmother said that too, my, my.
My what?

I gave my daughter a cat, she was two.
Cat, she said. Then: My cat.
My this. Myth is. No one owns, is owned, is own,
cat not less. It disappears
with a twitch of its tail
nonetheless real

into the forest of its
own story. I have done my best,
a feral person knows
taste of blood in the mouth
its own, not its own.
On the other side of the woods

maybe a tiger with burning coal eyes
or maybe a twitch. Rustle of leaves. No one.

Sam's

tired of no partner, wants
to snuzzle arse. Can't understand
a world of glass and sofas. Dreams
of feathers, fur, snapping bones,
taste of rancid meat. Doesn't like
the bland kibble, the canned boiled
beef. Gets stuck under the shed
chasing a cat. Howls. Howls at the
moon. Howls at people embracing
genteelly on the chairs. Needs
dead skunks, filth to roll in. Chases
birds across the sky, bumps hard
into the fence, birds fly on free
beyond him. Lies stunned blank
on the mowed lawn, can't understand
any of it.

Perhaps

*Do you think
the cat will come back?*

Dirty plates, debris of dinner,
day draining into the dirt
behind the rattan blind,

*Do you think
he will come back?*

A black disk-eyed cat
rises between us, his Stygian glare,
his fur sparkling in a thousand places—

Do you think?

Congealing fat on plates,
lukewarm coffee, cigarette butts
mashed in the spill—

Do you?

In the darkness down by the river, liquid cats
become their shadows. A luminous ellipse
slips in and out of trees.

The Home of the Radioactive Cats
(based on art by Sandy Skoglund)

in the home of the Radioactive Cats
an old trailer-dwelling couple
sets out supper, straight from the fridge
bread and cheese

the cats, glowing, green, rub against ankles
follow the old man
from the table to the rusty metal chair out front
on the makeshift porch
where he stokes his pipe

the cats, they're killing me anyway,
might as well smoke

the old woman scrapes off the plates
the cats play with the crusts
their bodies are almost transparent,
bulbous green muscles
arched green backs smooth green fur

(and here comes one now
delicate stealthy tread

(cautious ears
flattened against the head

(dreamcat, what are you doing here in the real?

"Girl Making a Garland"
Hans Suess von Kulmback, German, ca. 1480-1522

She sits inside the open window,
long blonde hair flowing over the shoulders
of her orange gown. She looks down, calm, intent.
Above her a banner scrolls
"Ich pint mit vergis mein nit,"
I bind with
forget-me-nots.

Her wooden hoop drips flowers.
A white cat sits on the outside sill,
focused as she, but on
something in the foreground we don't see.
A single flower lies on the sill
but the cat cares nothing for it.
The cat is scraggly, no one's

pampered pet, he looks a little sad.

This is a painting of desire,
of the twin desires to capture and be free.
(Her lover waits for her in another painting.)
The frame of the window does not constrain
either girl or cat, each of whom
could any minute leap out,

run down the cobbled streets. But there
they stay, in yellow sixteenth century sunlight,

she weaving a crown of tiny flowers,
he watching the road.

Unsent Letter to a Long Gone Friend

Remember the Shakespeare party? I the third
Ophelia in a borrowed dress, worried about
The red wine. Ann said, "If that's Jean's dress
Anything that could possibly happen to it
Already has." I did spill the crab dip,
You got it all out with carbon tet
In the workshop. But then your cat came in
Yowling, ear ripped. I said I would wash it
With green soap in the workshop sink, and did.
Got blood, mine and the cat's, on the beaded sleeves.

The cleaner did repairs too. Jean said only
How sorry she was she'd missed it. It's not true
That drinking brings nostalgia, what it is
Is, the nostalgia brings back drinking, sweat
On the last brown bottle, the beer I said
Would be my last. And was. I see it now
On the scarred boards of your ersatz dining-table,
Luminous as the grail.

5 A.M.

i

in dark trees:
flutterings, the aspen's
tiniest castanets.
winds murmur of heights and distances.

in the corner of your vision
the night's dead set sail toward God,
the tide takes them.

blue-grey forms
ghost the depths.

ii

mist rolls across the road,
my neighbor's house is three gold blurs
in the dark. webs trisect my face,
cling to my arms. the air smells damp
and green.

unseen pampas grass grazes
my arm. I try to find the drive
with my feet, it eludes me,
leaves slicken the lawn

but I am surefooted as a cat,

I think, till my cat slips by my ankle:
not true, he is surer of foot.

on the drive at last, my footsteps ring out.
trees hunch into the road, their dark bulk
a comfort. an old truck rattles past
spraying gravel, the daily paper sails out
to land with a plop at my feet.

my son says I am a ghost
crossing the yard in my white cotton gown,
no feet, no arms, no head.

the white paper is waving
a signal.

iii

the hour before the dawn,
that blue magician.

My Son Requests a Typewriter

13, he wants to write.
Not the computer he says, he wants
a typewriter. One of the first electrics
sleeps in the garage, I wipe the dust off
and plug it in. A hum. The ribbon, of course,
is dead. I order one.

The computer for now, I say. But he says no,
he waits for days. The ribbon comes,
we figure it out, what tab goes under what.
Now he is writing stories, typing away
in the back room.

I like to use the typewriter he says.
I like the way the clicks keep telling me
I'm writing something, it's moving along.
I like to x things out and see them still there
under the x's. I like the way the keys
push back against my fingers. I just like it.

The sound of key strokes in the other room,
as though they're in my head. As though I'm writing
my stories, the ones I am living,
the story of my making dinner,
the story of my feeding the cat,
the story of my walking the dog.

Look at this! he says.
The uneven type. The strikeouts.
`The End' in caps.

Flowering Cactus

on the front lawn
prickly pear grown wild in rainy weather—
like spiny driftwood, a gala float abandoned
from the elf parade, with papery yellow flowers

sweet scent, paid for by sharp pain

why not mow over it? gallant pirate ship
with all flags flying, queening it on the
sea of green

dogs and cats stay clear
it flashes yellow, yellow in the passing motorist's eye
a child reaches out her hand, once only—

still the mower stops again at the edge
of the tiny fortress,
its flags and spires aligned in green rebellion

backs off,
veers left, describes an uncharted arc

Still

In the attic, a framed photograph,
your retirement, all those smiling men.
I left it there, how could I have?
The suits, the ties, the formal farewell,
Your grey face.

Father.

Comes in, staggers against the lamp
An unfolding of maps.
Drunk, long dead,
the shadow of your pen
underwrites these lines.
There is a bright point where the two tips meet.

Your hand against the wall, a menagerie.
Seven different voices.
This is what the horse says.
This is what the hen says.

Where you were in the house: tinkle of ice in the glass.
I raise my O'Doul's to you.
Alone in the kitchen you paid for.

The animals were dark, they had to be,
but I remember them as moving lights,
the room a shadow.

What to do with the Remains

I want to be vaporized, like the old guy
Who would not leave his home at Mount St. Helens.
Not a trace left. No ashes to be thrown into
The Mediterranean, or even sprinkled in the hollow
Where I fed feral cats. Certainly
No formaldehyde, no box.
Just fly me over the nearest active volcano
And toss me in. Let there be nothing but molecules
To be breathed in by wild animals,
Causing them no distress,
Returning me to the air.

Facebook

a loud party
and all the neighbors home.
Here is Obama, there is
a cat in a dog suit, growling.
Sally just got
a speeding ticket! Imagine!
Blue blocks cascade
over pink ones and
a happy drunk glides by on skis.
Someone sends me a sheep
but it is too loud,
the colors are yelling. New bars
pop up, wink, and open,
inviting me to join.

Walking Home Late Sestina

The dull party is over and now after
we guests have slipped into the growing dark
we are tired, complaining, wondering if all
the shadows in the bushes are just cats.
We think so but are nervous. Are
after dark all cats perceived as gray—

a featureless, innocuous gray?
Rustlings in the background, after
bourbon and chatter are over, we are
not sure. In this part of the country it gets dark
early. Most of us have cats,
part of our ambiance. We are all—

except sniffly allergic Ralph—we are all
fond of cats, and we ourselves are gray.
Daytime and evening too. Neighborhood cats
appear and disappear. After
all, some things are visible in the dark,
like cats' eyes in the headlights. We are

not sure at night of who we really are.
Personae fall away, we are all
dissolved, old children playing in the dark,
our footsteps light although our heads are gray.
We call across the hedges, and after

Shouting goodbye, wonder if we hear cats

or not, maybe our younger selves, not cats,
as we used to be, not as now we are
in the quiet tepid hours after
the light grows dim. No answers here at all.
The world presents itself in shades of gray
before it simply deepens into dark.

We should be now acquainted with the dark
and know the moving darkness is not cats,
the dusk that comes is more than gray-on-gray.
You pluck my sleeve, you stammer, "Are
you ready?" For what comes? To bid it all
goodnight? Greet the hereafter?

And is the party over, though it's dark?
Our lost selves slip through shadows like those cats.
And after all we are, like them, dusk-gray.

Self-inflating Pillow
> "Perfect for the beach or the plane—just slip it into your purse."

Flat rubber fills itself with air.
The cat backs off, arches to stare.

A roundness gathers, wrinkles dim.
Cat slinks away—it's not for him.

What is it then? Fat CEO
Draining his workers' blood with no

Compunction, or corrupt cop
Involved in mammoth coverup—

Will it become a giant tick
And burst, to cover us with ick,

Or will it exhale itself flat?
It's round and slick. It scares the cat.

Sound of No Hands Clapping

Is God in the trill of the dawn songbird,
Or is God in the cat that kills the bird,

Or the dog that kills the cat,
Or the farmer that shoots the dog

On his way to the henhouse, or is God
In the machine that kills the farmer—

Deus in machina, or is God in the
Moments of full life only, subliminal flashes

Between the trill and the machine's crank,
The cry of beauty and the infinite silence?

Doors That Don't Quite Shut

The screen door didn't, but slammed
with a tinny bang and popped right back
open. Also the main wooden door
was warped, you could get it shut
but it was complicated and you didn't.
Dinner on the patio, steak and corn,
lounge chairs of plastic strips, and
conversation punctuated by those tinny
bangs. Bedroom and bathroom doors
didn't catch. You sang in the bathroom,
bedroom had protocol: "Ya in there?"
The cat could come in or the dog
without announcement, they brought solace.
I wasn't used to a house of solid doors,
of square rooms and rigid right angles.
All these keys, so many uncompromising
locks. I bang on all my doors
but I don't think I'm home.

A Rose by Any Other Name is Something Else

The austere nominalist
believes only particular concrete objects
exist. The items on the round table
do not constitute breakfast

although he slices the lid off the egg
and dips the spoon. How fully here one is
in a world of things, he says
to the cat. This cup of coffee

resembles nothing, you can not
rant or rhapsodize
in a world of no properties.
The African violet is neither

beautiful nor trite, accepts no
comparison, the cat itself
is just the cat, unhaunted
by catness. The austere

nominalist frowns, he brushes
individual crumbs away, the world

will not assemble. Ah, and yet life
is simplicity itself.

Solo

you can sleep with all the cats you want
and have a breakfast for dinner
and talk on the phone for two hours with your best friend

you can take the dog for a midnight walk
and make cappuchino and not clean out the machine
and play solitaire on the computer

and order pizza with ham and pineapple
and have a dinner for breakfast
and skip lunch

you can stay up all night reading
you don't have to yield or compromise
on anything

you can do anything legal you want
and some illegal things
because no one is watching

so why then do you want him to come home?

Review Copy

I liked your first poems
      before you learned
how to hide so well in them,

    that friendly
intimate casual ambiance:
    spilled coffee, a cat curled up

on a dirty sweatshirt.
    How good it felt
to thumb our nose at the sonnet,

the war, the world.
    This must in fact be coffee,
 this dark blotch on the cover,

it has a sweetish-sour smell
      (even after twenty years)
like friendly sweat.

absence in the new book teases:
        pawprint next to the overturned
           begonia, crisp pages,

spaces whistling between
    words, you must have been there,

been here, but always too quickly
for me.

Explanation

out there at night:
tiny pairs of eyes
in the azaleas,
behind the privet.

I used to think
cats' eyes gave off light,
did not reflect
headlights, streetlamps.

few natural things
will shine like that,
but here there are
no cats.

those lucent points,
then, in darkness, those
are ghostcats. cats
gassed, shot,

hit by trucks, mauled by
coyotes, cats that never knew
fireside and couch,
a human hand.

these cats have names,
shadowwind, willothewisp,
stalkreed, featherbreath.
stand in your lighted

doorway and call them.
one by one
they shut their eyes
and disappear.

Narrow Places

narrow places,
train cars squeezed to half size
and accelerating, snowy crevasses
opening underfoot,
tall thin rooms in the house
I did not know were there

* * *

Last night one of the cats turned out to be a tiger cub. He had been diagnosed as such by the doctor, who said he would have to be caught and either killed or put in the zoo. I was frantically trying to find a place for him in a zoo, calling one after another, being told that they had enough tigers and could not take him, being given other numbers. Meanwhile he was outside, striding round the glassed in porch, all white, bigger every time I saw him but absolutely beautiful, sun on white fur with muscles moving underneath.

* * *

In the boring meeting, the white acoustic tiles in the ceiling, which I always count, began to turn black. They would get grayer and grayer, one by one, until they were completely black. I knew that once the entire ceiling was black we would all die. The Department Head was talking about initiatives and twenty-year plans and he had Powerpoint slides with jagged rising graphs. I raised my hand and tried to get his attention, but I was unable to. The tiles continued to turn black, until there were just four of them, a square, right over my head. Everyone else seemed frozen in place, the Head's hand extended, someone stopped in the middle of removing his glasses. The last four tiles started to turn gray all at once.

* * *

If you go free, my soul
what place is left for you to roam
under trees, down by the river
behind the poisoned house?

2012
> (when, according to the Mayan calendar, the
> world will end)

on the last day I would
knowing it was the last day knowing
there would be no more of time
no more afternoon on the deck with the cat
and the birds and the leaves falling slowly
knowing there would be no one to tell
it to and no one to tell it
no one to say: I remember the line of black
edging across the sky or: I should not have
wasted so much of my time in bitterness
and no cat to stroke who is lying
on the picnic table and feeling
the warmth of the sun on her old skin
I would nevertheless go out
as I just did go out and sweep the leaves
from the deck and stroke the old cat and
although there would be no evening
and no one to say goodbye to
no goodbye because of its being the end
the real end not just another imagined end
I would pick up my pen and I would write

Movement, Solitude, Space

Waking with a cat
Next to you, is comfort—
She is not a threat or an obligation
And is complete in herself,
Has no need of you or
Anyone, though she is happy
With your company. She yawns languidly
And grooms herself. Perhaps you might like
To get up.

* * *

I know it is quite wrong
To let the water drip in the sink for the cat
But I do it sometimes
She gives a joyous leap
Into the bowl and I imagine
What it is for her:
A great hole in the sky
And the purest essence
Falling drop by drop before your nose
And you're thirsty

* * *

Cat people do not demand love
Or give it well, they are more used to

Wary friendship. A shared meal,
Your rights respected and mine, and the distance
Between us. There is the cold fresh call
Of the moon, starlight on the rough
Singled roof. The distance.

* * *

My best friend feared and
Hated cats. I had to lock them away
Before she came. Once one escaped
And she ran screaming. On TV
We saw the Tasmanian Devils on the nature channel.
They howled and bit each other and stripped
The land right down to the dirt. That is what cats
Are like, she said, underneath.

* * *

Sleep has withdrawn her webs,
Nothing between you and the night sky.
The window is open
And the planets wheel over you.
How temporary you are!
The cat rolls, stretches.

At the Liendo
Hempstead, Texas, August 2004

Lunch at the grand old house turned restaurant,
wide porches, scrawled menu-slate,
flagstone walk, hedges and shrubs, wildflowers–

and a dozen cats and kittens on the porches,
snoozing in groups, nosing kibble, chasing
invisible insects over the varnished boards–

and we play with them, half tame, half feral,
letting us touch, but arched and poised to run,
until it's our turn to sit on bentwood chairs,

be fed etouffe and sweet tea, and talk
of past good times, while now and then at windows
a tiny face appears and vanishes.

I don't want to know what will happen after.
I want to think that life can just spread out
sometimes, sleepy and shiny, voluptuous,

cats, green jasmine, trumpet vine, mint.

Sleeping Women in Movies

She is sprawled arms akimbo
    Yawns and stretches luxuriously
In black and white, tosses a satin pillow
Or she is curled on a lush divan
    Shrugs off the cat
        Reaches for her cell phone playing Bach
Or she wakens to a bird call, a slant of light
        Rubs from her eyes the shreds of dream
            Pads to the kitchen in her bunny slippers

Ah, to enact sleep,
    Its accouterments,
        Its ebbing tide
Your tresses spread over the bed's edge—

To fall asleep to, and to wake to, fiction—

The Cat at the End of That Poetry Anthology

the striped cat is at the garbage pail
on the last page of the book
average cat, standard pail. his paw poking
a greasy paper bag of tin cans
and crumpled paper; you can smell
a rich sardiny smell of the seventies
wafting down the gray alley
where he's come
from mating and prowling
hungry

his delicate step certain
on all uneasy surfaces
mattress spring
hanging bird feeder
cyclone fence
window box
where they are planting grass
in sweaty summer bedrooms
sheets slick with pizza and love

Tom-of-the alley
archback surefoot

not afraid to touch
and oh, that beautiful rancid freedom

Monastery Cats

3, black and white,
gray, brindled, jump
to the kitchen window ledge
at San Lorenzo di Brindisi.

the hills around Rome are fading
and a single orange
falls from the tree
into the herb garden.

in a lighted square
a woman at the sink,
hair covered with
white restraining cap.

what is here is what
has always been here,
cloth, dishpan,
chalice, beaker, spoon,

matins, vespers. cats
rub against the window,
she puts the scraps out
in the last light,

from my dormitory window,
maybe a quarter mile away
I think I hear their purring,
her singing.

www.ingramcontent.com/pod-product-compliance
Lightning Source LLC
Chambersburg PA
CBHW020946090426
42736CB00010B/1289